A Library
Comes to Town

by Juan Lester

illustrated by David Shelton

PEARSON

Scott Foresman

Editorial Offices: Glenview, Illinois • Parsippany, New Jersey • New York, New York
Sales Offices: Needham, Massachusetts • Duluth, Georgia • Glenview, Illinois
Coppell, Texas • Ontario, California • Mesa, Arizona

ISBN: 0-328-13229-2

Jane and her father walked down the
street. They saw a bookstore. Her father
looked in the window. Then he sighed.
 "Why are you unhappy?" asked Jane.

"I love to read all different kinds of books," answered Jane's father. "But books cost a lot of money. "

"Are we too poor to buy books?" asked Jane.

"We are not poor, but we are not rich," said her father. "Only rich people can buy most books."

"That's unfair," said Jane. "I wish there was a way that everyone could have books to read."

"My dear child, I agree," said her father.

A week later, Jane was helping her brothers repaint some old chairs. As she worked, Jane could hear some neighbors talking.

What she heard made her very happy. She went running into the house to tell her father.

"Father!" she cried. "A man named Ben Franklin is going to open a library in town. You do not have to be rich to borrow books from the library!"

"That is a great thing," said her father. "Noww people can read all the books they want and carry them home!"

Ben Franklin

Ben Franklin opened up the first public library in the United States. This was over 200 years ago. He wanted to make sure that everyone could have books to read. He also came up with other "firsts."

Ben Franklin invented swimming fins, a stove, and a special kind of reading glasses. All these are things that people still use today.